A Lime, a Mime, a Pool of Slime

More about Nouns

To Noreen
　　—B.P.C.

A Lime, a Mime, a Pool of Slime

More about Nouns

by Brian P. Cleary

illustrations by Brian Gable

M̲ MILLBROOK PRESS / MINNEAPOLIS

A jet is a noun,

and so is Peru.

Friend is a noun, and so is your dad,

ice cream
and bagels
and Boston

and Brad.

QUINCY MARKET

Bost

If it's a
hippo,
house,
or ham,

COACH

if it's your coach,
a roach,
or ram,

if it's a rock,
a clock, or clown,
then—oh my gosh, Josh—
it's a noun!

And so is a comma and your momma, a billy goat a baby llama,

COMMA

a doorway, Norway,
hand-me-downs—
    all the things you see
are nouns.

If it's a person,
place,
or thing,
a palace,
pal,

or shiny bling,

12

a shack or sheriff
in your town,

it's fundamental—
it's a noun!

But there are **nouns**
you cannot touch
or smell or hear or see.

This type is called an
abstract noun,
like joy and harmony.

Love and hate are abstract nouns, and so are peace and hope.

You cannot taste or hold them, like a tart or telescope.

Proper nouns
all name specific
people, things, and places.

Like Uncle Lou

or Timbuktu,

they start with upper cases.

Like Mallory or Valerie, the Seventeenth Street Gallery,

Pizza Pete's and Ming's Chinese,

proper nouns name each of these.

Or Brannigan and Flannigan, parading in with Anne again.

Whether they're **abstract** or proper or neither,

whether it's talent or Timmy or teether,

if it can be thought about,

ridden uptown,

talked to, or walked to,
it's surely a noun!

Like beagle
or eagle,
a robin
or wren,

a breeze,
a sneeze,
a scary mime.

Nouns are words like
girls and curls,
cats and flats,

FLATS

HEELS

and hats
and pearls.

A crumb, some gum,
a tiny rocket—

a noun can be
what's in your pocket.

If it's a **tape** or **DVD**,

a **teacher's aide** or **Germany**,

a coat that's made of

wool
or down,

then say it with me—
it's a noun!

So, what is a noun?

Do you know?

ABOUT THE AUTHOR & ILLUSTRATOR

BRIAN P. CLEARY is the author of the Words Are CATegorical©, Math Is CATegorical©, Adventures in Memory™, and Sounds Like Reading™ series. He has also written The Laugh Stand: Adventures in Humor; Peanut Butter and Jellyfishes: A Very Silly Alphabet Book; The Punctuation Station; and two poetry books. Mr. Cleary lives in Cleveland, Ohio.

BRIAN GABLE is the illustrator of several Words Are Categorical™ books, the Math Is Categorical™ series, and the Make Me Laugh! joke books. He lives in Toronto, Ontario.

Text copyright © 2006 by Brian P. Cleary
Illustrations copyright © 2006 by Lerner Publishing Group, Inc.

Millbrook Press
A division of Lerner Publishing Group, Inc.
241 First Avenue North
Minneapolis, MN 55401 U.S.A.

Website address: www.lernerbooks.com

Library of Congress Cataloging-in-Publication Data

Cleary, Brian P., 1959—
    A lime, a mime, a pool of slime : more about nouns / by Brian P. Cleary ; illustrations by Brian Gable.
        p.   cm. — (Words Are Categorical)
    ISBN 978-1-57505-937-2 (lib. bdg. : alk. paper)
    ISBN 978-0-8225-7184-1 (eBook)
    1. English language—Noun—Juvenile literature. I. Gable, Brian, 1949—
II. Title.
PE1201.C577 2006
428.1—dc22   2005025888

Manufactured in the United States of America
7 — BP — 2/1/13